I0235023

IMAGES
of America

MILLVILLE

These scenes show Third Street just east of Sherman Avenue in Millville in the 1930s. (KH.)

On the Cover: Millville workers are assembled for a photograph at the shipyard in 1920. Many Millville residents probably can point out an ancestor among these shipbuilders. Charlie Silcox in the white shirt and dark vest is at the right center of the ramp; Stuart A. Pratt is second from right on the ramp, and his father, A. L. Pratt, is on the top row, far right. (AC.)

IMAGES
of America

MILLVILLE

Ann Pratt Houpt

ARCADIA
PUBLISHING

Copyright © 2005 by Ann Pratt Houpt
ISBN 978-1-5316-1232-0

Published by Arcadia Publishing
Charleston, South Carolina

Library of Congress Catalog Card Number: 2005921536

For all general information contact Arcadia Publishing at:
Telephone 843-853-2070
Fax 843-853-0044
E-mail sales@arcadiapublishing.com
For customer service and orders:
Toll-Free 1-888-313-2665

Visit us on the Internet at www.arcadiapublishing.com

Dedicated to the Anderson and Jasperson cousins

The fishing boat *John Henry Sherman*, shown *c.* 1923 at Millville, was built in 1921 at the Sherman Shipyard. The boat was lost in the 1929 hurricane in the Tortugas (Florida Keys), where coral cut the bottom of the boat out according to notes by Bill Frederickson. (MFS/BFC.)

CONTENTS

ACKNOWLEDGMENTS

The author acknowledges the help of many persons in gathering the photographs for *Millville*.

Marjorie Arnold was helpful, especially in contacting the heart of Millville—its school. Diane Hall and Bobbie Kochevar helped kick off research into the history of the community. Out-of-town former Millville residents Donna Houser, Judy Williams, and Harold Jasperson spent time on the phone and sent photographs. Martha Suggs provided the photographs in the collection of her late father, Bill Frederickson. Verniece Rogers Millis provided pictures, including the Teen Timers's photographs. Rebecca Wallace, president of the Bay County Historical Society, was a tremendous support, as always, and Anita Lucas provided patient help with the library local history materials.

This is an early aerial photograph of Millville showing Watson Bayou, the lumberyard docks, railroad tracks, and roads. (BCPL.)

INTRODUCTION

Northwest Florida was truly a frontier area when Millville first became a community, situated on the point of land bordered by Watson Bayou and St. Andrews Bay. Watson Bayou was named for the family that bought the land at the entrance to the bayou, with other large tracts for lumbering purposes in 1834 and 1835. James B. Watson erected a mill on one of the points. The lumber mill changed hands several times.

Destruction of all property along the shore during the Civil War brought business of all kinds to an end. The first settler after the war was William Holmes who arrived in 1869 with his family. He bought a schooner and engaged in the Pensacola and St. Andrews Bay trade, building larger vessels as his need demanded. For years, the area depended on sailing vessels and wagons from Jackson County to bring in supplies.

In 1886, Henry Bovis and associates began building a lumber mill at the head of Watson Bayou and named it the St. Andrews Lumber Company. It attracted workers who constructed a town around the mill. Several families had organized a Sunday school about 1886 and built a small schoolhouse. They also formed the Watson Bayou Literary Society, which met at the school.

The future looked bright at the turn of the century. Millville developed into the industrial and commercial center of the area. Bovis sold his lumber company to a foreign syndicate, and it became the German-American Lumber Company. Hundreds moved to Millville to work at the big lumber mill. Most of the workers were paid in scrip, to be spent at the big company store.

An article in the January 16, 1908, issue of the *Panama City Pilot* newspaper describes the history of "the thriving little town of Millville."

A post office was soon established and officially named Millville. Bovis had been looking over pinelands in this section of the county for some time and had acquired a large tract of timber. The lumber mill had a capacity of about 20,000 feet per day. Bovis, Milligan, and Adams operated the mill under the name St. Andrews Bay Lumber Company. Adams soon left however, and Bovis and Milligan continued to operate the mill until they sold it to the German-American Lumber Company (G.A.L.). This company incorporated in 1901 with a capital of $250,000 and rebuilt the mill, giving it a capacity of 80,000 feet per day. They modernized with a large dry kiln and a planing mill. The *Pilot* reported that the mill was entirely destroyed by fire on December 19, 1906. Ground was broken for a new mill in February 1907, and it started manufacturing lumber again the following September. This newly improved mill included two band saws and edgers, and it could turn out staves, headings, pickets, and shingles. Adjoining is a large planing mill and a well-equipped machine shop. The company's electric light plant produced lighting for both the mill and the town. It also included a large reservoir.

The new mill had a capacity of 100,000 feet per day and was reported to have secured land to produce enough timber to last 25 years. The company operated about 50 miles of logging road, equipped with 4 locomotives, 35 log cars, and 15 camp cars. Output of the mill was shipped on barges to Pensacola and sent from there to points in Germany and South America.

The lumber company operated a general mercantile store, which was reported in 1908 to be doing a business of over $60,000 per year. They operated the tug *Dewey* used on St. Andrews Bay for towing logs, handling lumber, and delivering freight. The company also owned 100 tenement houses.

The town grew up around the lumber mills and shipyards. By 1911, there were six general stores, two grocery stores, a drug store, a millinery, a livery, and a turpentine operation in Millville, in addition to the German-American Lumber Company.

In 1913, the citizens voted in favor of incorporation and elected W. I. Singletary mayor. Other city officers were W. W. Mashburn, clerk, and Jack Stone, the first town marshall. The first group of seven aldermen included S. T. Ward, J. J. Holmes, R. D. Prows, C. C. McClure, R. F. Ennis, S. E. Harsey, and F. M. Turner, according to Harold Bell in *Glimpses of the Panhandle*.

The 1920 census showed Millville with a population of 1,887 people, still the largest town on St. Andrews Bay, but it was being overtaken by an area just to the west called Panama City.

Florida governor John W. Martin called a special session of the legislature in November 1925 during which Bay County representative J. Ed Stokes introduced a bill to combine the three separate municipalities of Millville, St. Andrews, and Panama City into a single larger one to be known as Panama City. In 1926, the cities of Millville, Bay Harbor, and St. Andrews were annexed into the incorporated limits of Panama City.

KEY TO PHOTOGRAPH COURTESY ABBREVIATIONS

AC: Author's Collection
BCPL: Bay County Public Library
LJB: Lana Jane Brent
SB: Steven Bruner
JHC: Janet Harrison Carter
JAC: Jeri Anderson Clemmons
RC: Ralph Conrad
CFC: Cotton Family Collection (Peggy Malone, Bobbie Kochevar, and Deanne Coffield)
FLC: Frederick Casey, Boyette and Casey Hardware Company
RF: Rev. Harvey and Rose Ferrell Collection
GFC: Odeal Gainer, Gainer Family Collection
BFC: Bill Frederickson Collection

IBC: Immanuel Baptist Church
GG: Glenn Gibbs Collection loaned to BCPL
KH: Kathryn Hanline
JSH: Jacqueline Sorensen Hogan
DPH: Donna Pratt Houser
MH: Diane and Michelle Hall
HJ: Harold Jasperson
DAR: Ann Johnson Robbins
DYM: Donna Youngblood Mattern
VRM: Verniece Rogers Millis
RP: Mr. and Mrs. Russell Phillips
MFS: Martha Frederickson Suggs
JW: Judy Williams
FA: Fellowship Academy
LS: Lois Spiva

Trees on the shore frame a view of this four-master anchored in Watson Bayou Harbor. (MS/BFC.)

One

SHIPYARDS AND
LUMBER MILLS

In 1912, this Millville street looked like any frontier town. At the turn of the century, the whole area around St. Andrews Bay was a frontier. Millville grew up around its lumber mills and shipyards as the center of commerce in the bay area. At right is the German-American Lumber Company. The building at left is the Millville Supply Company, a general merchandise and hardware store owned by W. B. Gray. Millville Masonic Lodge met upstairs. Other businesses nearby included E. E. Van Horn's Restaurant and Rooming House and a confectionery store owned by the Russell Prows family, according to Harold Bell in *Glimpses of the Panhandle*. (BCPL.)

W. I. Singletary was the first mayor of Millville, which did not incorporate into a town until July 1913. He also was a charter member of the Millville Baptist Church and one of the organizers of the Millville Chamber of Commerce. (IBC.)

Six unidentified Millville citizens stand in front of a furniture and clothing store c. 1904. This is reported to be Will Gray's store. The town hall was upstairs. (BCPL.)

Third Street in summer 1907 still had shade trees growing in the right of way. C. E. and C. S. Russ owned the Russ Brothers General Merchandise, which was located just above the railroad tracks on Third Street in Millville. (BCPL.)

The Home Bakery is shown in the left foreground of this view of Third Street looking west. By 1910, when this photograph was made, Millville's population was the largest of any of the towns on St. Andrews Bay. (BCPL.)

Unidentified employees of St. Andrews Bay Lumber Company pose for a photograph in front of the company store. (BCPL.)

Charlie Powell, left, and Jim Daffin stand ready to serve customers at the soda fountain in the company store. (BCPL.)

St. Andrews Bay Lumber Co.'s Department Store, Millville, Fla.

The company store, located at the corner of what is now Sherman Avenue and east Third Street, provided for the needs of the company's workmen and their families. (BCPL.)

The Confectionery and Palm Room, Millville, Fla.

This photograph is from a 2¢ postcard showing the Confectionery and Palm Room in the Old Prows Building on the corner of Sherman Avenue and Third Street in 1916. The building burned sometime between 1925 and 1930. Later Dr. Stenson's Drug Store was located there. (BCPL.)

W. C. Sherman purchased the German-American Lumber Company when the federal government offered it for sale to private owners in 1919. He formed the St. Andrews Bay Lumber Company, which included lumber mills and a shipyard. (BCPL.)

W. C. Sherman is standing at left with his workers at the lumber company. (GG.)

Shown here are Edith Coppedge Pickens and her husband, Peter Zeno Pickens, who was a foreman at the German-American Lumber Company and a dredge operator for the building of the Dixie Sherman Hotel. (BCPL, loaned by Georgia Thomas Henry-Pearson.)

Peter Zeno Pickens (standing, second from left wearing a suit) is shown here with a group of railroad workers. (BCPL, loaned by Georgia Thomas Henry-Pearson.)

The shipbuilding crew is gathered for the launching of either the *John Henry Sherman* or the *JH Laird* at Sherman Shipyard in 1921. (AC.)

Moore Lumber Company's Bay Harbor sawmill was in operation from 1912 to 1924, when it burned. The mill stood west of East Avenue at the foot of the bridge. The log pond was east of the bridge. (BCPL.)

Two ships are on the ways, located between the carpenter shop, off to the left, and the warehouse, shown at right. (MFS.)

This photograph of Sherman Shipyard in the mid-1920s was taken from across Watson Bayou. (MFS.)

Shown are men working on a four-masted vessel, the *Tempate*, the first ship docked on the marine ways at Sherman Shipyard in 1920. A. L. Pratt is at center, holding his hat. (AC.)

This is a view of the *Tempate* on the main ways at left and the *Guna Caste* (?) afloat. A note on the back of the photograph inserted the question mark; it is unknown if the note's author was unsure of the ship's name or the correct spelling. (MFS/BFC.)

W. C. Sherman stands on the bow of the *Martha S* in 1937. Bill Frederickson is at right on the afterdeck. This vessel was built at the shipyard in Millville about 1920 and was rebuilt in 1936. (MFS.)

The steamer *Dewey*, shown on dry dock in 1908, was 68 feet in length and 3 feet in depth. In towing service, it was used on the bay towing logs, handling lumber barges between local points, and delivering freight, according to the *Panama City Pilot* in January 1908. The *Dewey* was built in 1899 in Portland, Florida. (MFS.)

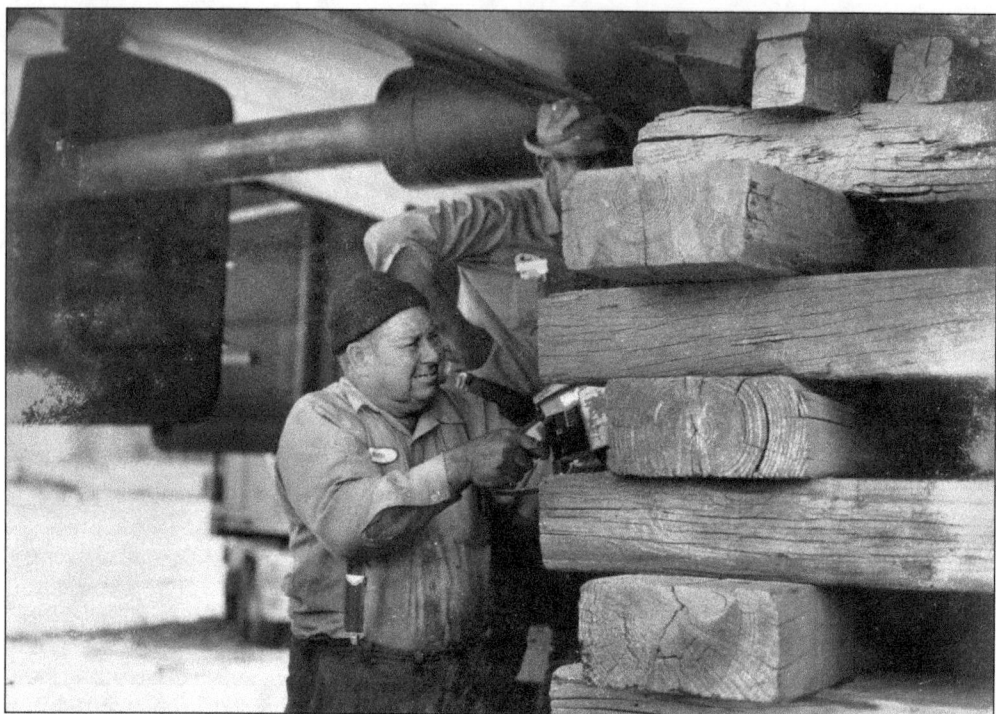

The Sherman Shipyard continued service in shipping. Here Bill Frederickson is shown cutting out blocks. (MFS.)

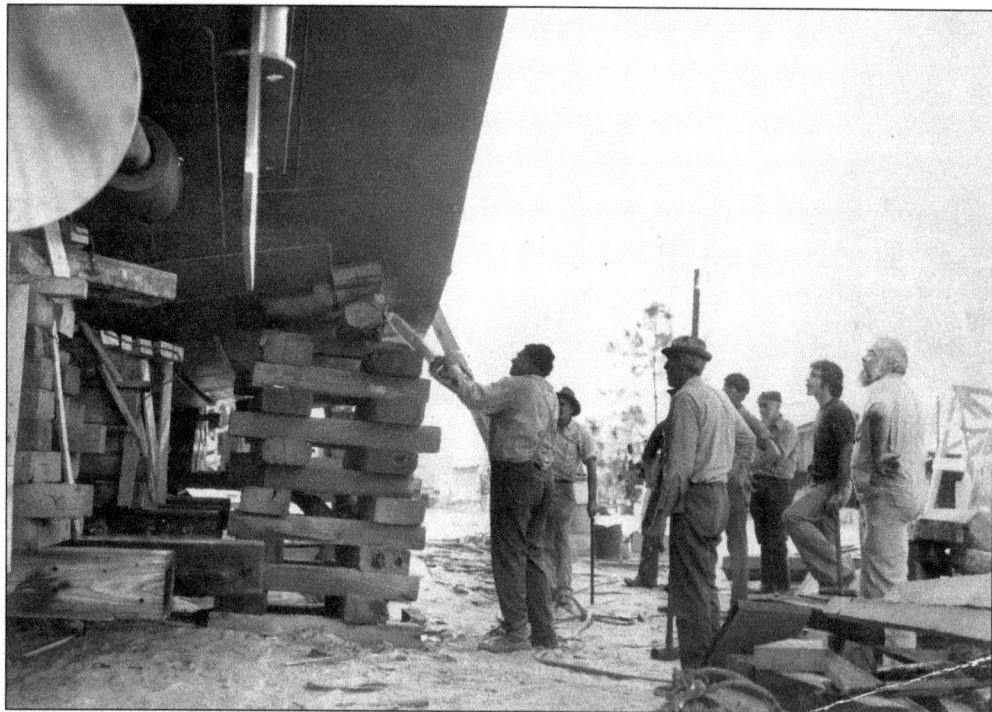

Frederickson, left;, Rufus Griffin; Julian Harrison, right foreground; and a crew of workers in February 1976 are shown cutting out blocks to launch a new vessel, the LASH *Express*. (MFS.)

This is the LASH (lighter aboard ship) *Express* built in Sherman Shipyard and launched February 25, 1976, according to notes on the back of the picture. This is an example of the 22 modern all-steel tugs built at the shipyard in Millville through the 1980s. (MFS.)

The *Sherman VI* was built at Sherman Shipyard in 1941. Bill Frederickson wrote on the back of the photograph that he laid the keel, helped build, planked, and launched the hull in five weeks. Capt. Alex Ceruti was foreman, and the workers included John Tomas, master shipwright; Frederickson, ship carpenter; Fred Seaborn and Charlie Parker, caulkers; C. P. Moates, Huey Lindsey, Paul S?, Porter Strickland, Dock Hodges, Sam Meredith, Sam Burkett, L. Stubbs, A. Brown, and A. Brown, carpenters; Cecil S?, Alford Lee Hutto, Greg Williams, and Brown Spiva, apprentice carpenters. (MFS.)

This photograph of the paper mill smoke stack under construction was made *c.* 1930. Rev. Charles W. Odom (in center, with straw hat) and W. W. Kelly (in overalls with back to the camera) are both Parker residents. (BCPL.)

The note on back of this photograph says simply "working" and is dated 1921. The men appear to be clearing the land. (DPH.)

This postcard is a view of the paper mill taken in the mid-1930s or early-1940s. Note the dark smoke—over the years the mill has installed air and water pollution control measures. (BCPL.)

The first cargo of paper (1,600 tons) was shipped from International Paper Southern Kraft Mill on the Waterman Steamship Company's SS *Lillian*. The observers include Panama City mayor F. M. Nelson (fourth from left), J. Will Brown (fifth from left), Y. E. Smith (sixth from left), and A. J. Pelham (eighth from left). Waterman Steamship Company was local, with offices in Panama City. (BCPL.)

Clarence Silcox, left, is assisted in holding up a large bobcat by Homer Andrews c. 1920. This bobcat was killed by Silcox and Andrews while hunting; it was stuffed and was displayed in Fisher-Stinson Hardware Company in Panama City for many years. (KH.)

Enjoying a day of fishing on Pinelog Creek are Evelyn Silcox, left, and Honor King. Pinelog empties into the Choctawhatchee River. (KH.)

Two
FAMILIES

The Cotton family posed for this photograph in 1911. From left to right are Charles Jr., Eunice
Lavonia holding Eunice Elizabeth, Percy Scott, Charles Sr. holding Mary Belle, and Bernice Newton.
The person standing is unidentified. Mr. Cotton's friends teased him, saying, "Cotton would not
grow in Bay County." Cotton replied, "It looks like you'd know cotton does well, by looking at all
the little towheads running around my house." However, just for fun, he planted two rows of cotton
in the backyard to prove that cotton really would grow well in Bay County. (CFC.)

The Gray family, leaders in Millville history, is shown in this photograph from the collection of Ralph Conrad. J. C. Gray and his three sons, R. H. (back row, right), W. B. (front row, right), and J. S. (back row, left) and their families arrived in Millville in 1899 and began participating in community development. The women and other children are not identified. (RC.)

Eunice Lavonia Scott and Charles Cotton Sr. pose with their son Fitzhugh Lee Cotton c. 1902. (CFC.)

The Stone family is shown in 1925. Included are, from left to right, Jessie Lee Stone, Mary Stone (King), baby Edna Stone (Gibbs), Josie Stone, Coleman Stone (in back), Mattie Mae Stone (Brogdon), and Silas A. Stone. (GG.)

In June 1925, Mr. and Mrs. Joseph W. Fleming brought their family to Millville. They are shown with their daughter, Etta Belle, and sons Bill, James, and Paul. Joseph, who was ordained in Mississippi before he married, became a deacon in the Millville Baptist Church. (RC.)

In this photograph, it was noted that the two-story house looks as if it is one of the houses on Third Street. Standing in front are Emmie Shiry and Johnnie Stokes. (RP.)

Edmund Pratt and his wife, Wilhelmina Parker Pratt, who married April 2, 1905, are shown at their home on Maine Street in Millville c. 1910. He was employed at the shipyard. They had three children Harold, Huell, and Catherine. The Pratts sold the house about 1920 and bought Wilhelmina's family's home place on Martin Bayou. (DPH.)

Shown here *c.* 1910 are Millville residents Lillian Pratt Anderson, John Anderson, and their son, Harry. They owned the Millville Service Station at 320 Parher Highway, now Third Street. (DPH, from Arthur and Gertrude Pratt albums.)

This photograph probably was taken about 1917. The group includes several World War I soldiers. (RP.)

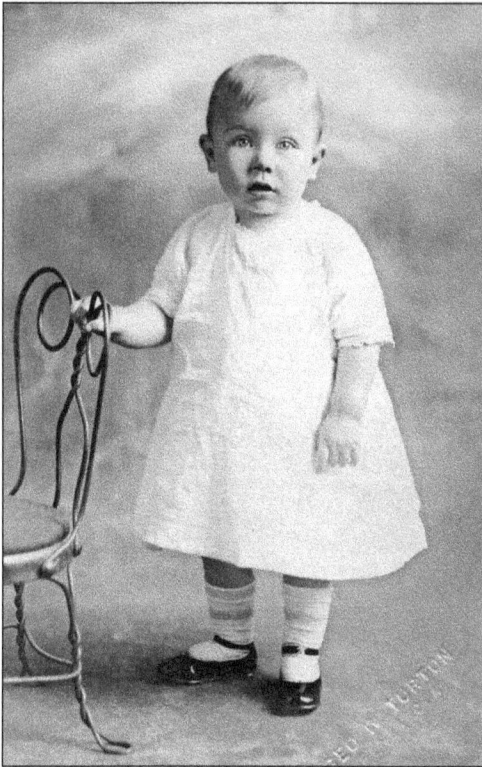

This is a photograph of Bill Frederickson in 1917 when well-dressed little boys wore beautiful white dresses and were right in style. (MFS.)

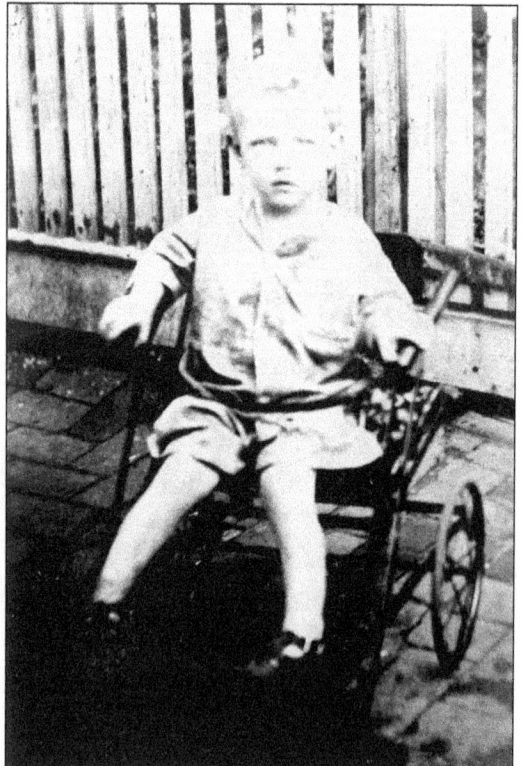

Hiram Conrad is shown in his wheelchair c. 1910 after being injured in an accidental fall. (RC.)

"Which one is Josie Cogburn?" is the note on this photograph. One of these two young ladies, Josie, became the wife of James Helton Harrison. They owned Harrison Mercantile in downtown Millville. (JHC.)

In this family group, James Harrison is second from right, and Josie Cogburn is third from right. (JHC.)

This is a photograph of John Phillips. It was probably taken at Mexico Beach in the 1930s. He worked at the German-American Lumber Company and later worked as a stevedore at the paper mill. (RP.)

Eunice Lavonia Scott Cotton happily holds her grandchildren. From left to right they are Christopher Charles, Barbara Louise, and John Arthur Cotton at the beach in 1936. (CFC.)

J. E. Jasperson, one of Jasper and Belle Jasperson's sons, stands behind a sporty car. (DPH.)

Mrs. Harold Jasperson is pictured with her son, Harold Jr., on June 30, 1938. (HJ.)

Bill Frederickson and his sister Dorothy Lagergren are pictured in 1935. (MFS.)

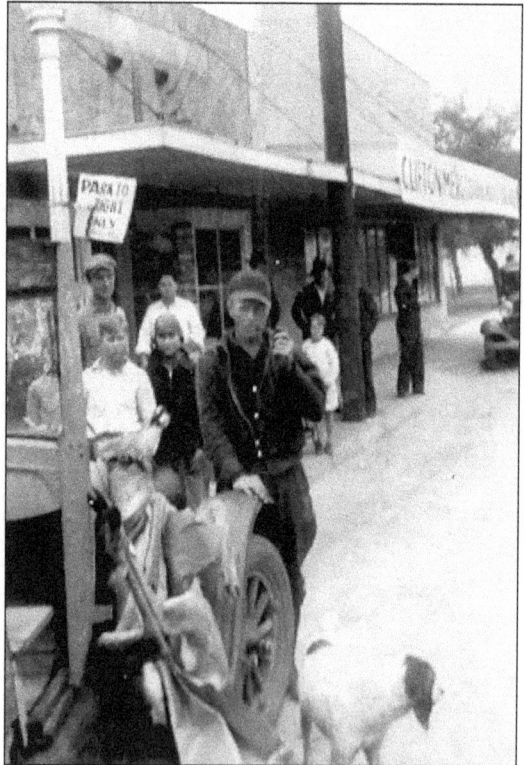

Clarence Augustus Silcox, with a deer and a dog, is standing in front of what is now Sweet Magnolia's on Third Street just east of Sherman Avenue in Millville, probably in the 1930s.

Members of the Cotton family relax on the porch of the Millville house c. 1938. They are from left to right (first row) Dorothy Eunice Cotton, bottom step; (second row) Anita Paige Bauler; (third row) Eunice Elizabeth (Cotton) Hutton, Eunice Lavonia Scott Cotton, Thelma Eunice Bauler, unidentified woman in the chair, Charles Cotton Jr., John Arthur Hutton, and Irma Hallford Cotton in the rocker holding Eunice Ann Hutton. (CFC.)

Mary Byrd and R. E. Youngblood are pictured here in the 1930s. R. E. recalled a time when Bay County was covered with massive cypress trees. In the 1920s, replanting was unheard of, and cypress was too slow growing. The county later was reforested with pines destined for pulp. (DYM.)

Robert G. Gainer and Odeal Carter Gainer pose with their six-month-old son, Gerald, in December 1942. (GFC.)

R. E. and Mary Youngblood are shown with their son, Dickie, and daughter, Donna, at their home in Millville about 1941. R. E. was a millwright at International Paper Company. (DYM.)

This photograph of Lula Mae and Walter Lewis Gainer was taken April 4, 1943, at Econfina Creek. The land the Gainer family homesteaded crossed the Econfina Creek. (GFC.)

Kinfolk gathered at the Jasperson home at 101 Springfield Avenue in Millville include from left to right (first row) Arthur L. Pratt; his sisters, Lillian Anderson, Belle Jasperson, and Hattie Williams; Lee Warren and daughter Betty Ann; and Jasper Jasperson; (second row) Martha Ann ?, Gertrude Pratt, and John Anderson. (HJ.)

Charles Silcox is seated between his sons, Clarence Augustus (left) and John W. (right), in about 1941. (KH.)

Evelyn Silcox, wife of Clarence Augustus Silcox, stands at right on the back row with her mother and sisters. From left to right they are (front row) Mary Jo, Kathleen, Isabel; (back row) Stella, Mary Wettstein, and Evelyn c. 1944. (KH.)

Pastor Harvey D. Ferrell and his wife, Rose, are shown in front of the Millville Assembly parsonage in 1944 with their children Jimmy, Danny, and Rosella, holding baby, Sammy. (RF.)

Members of the Jasperson family are gathered around a bicycle c. 1941. From left to right are (first row, on the bike) Betty Ann, Gwendolyn, and Harold Jr.; (second row) Lee Warren, Dorothy Jasperson, Jasper Sr., Glenn, Dorothy, and Belle Jasperson; (third row) Harold, and an unidentified child on his shoulders. (HJ.)

A family gathering includes from left to right Odeal and Bob Gainer, Olivia Carter, Cleatous Carter, Oveal Carter, and Gladys and Carl Carter. (GFC.)

Eunice Lavonia Scott Cotton is holding granddaughter Ira Janine King (left) and Virginia Gayle Cotton in 1946. (CFC.)

Among those attending a wedding party for Nellie Carter and Harold Hunt at the Dutch Girl Tavern, located at 2640 Coastal Highway in Millville, are from left to right (seated) Carl Carter, Cleatous Carter, four unidentified, Nellie Carter, Harold Hunt, Odeal Gainer, Bob Gainer, and Gladys Carter; and (standing) four unidentified. (GFC.)

Dempsey Barron, who grew up in Millville, is shown here with his first wife, Louverne, and their sons, Steve and Stuart. The photograph is a card with a message on the back from Barron to the 25th Senatorial District, which included Washington, Bay, Calhoun, and Gulf Counties, c. 1964. The card stated that he had served in the Florida Legislature for the past four years. He was elected to the Florida Senate in 1960 and served until 1988. He was president of the Senate from 1974 to 1976. (GG.)

41

All ready for Easter in 1952 are Bob and Odeal Gainer with their children (from left to right) Glenda, Ann, and Gerald. (GFC.)

Audrey Pressley gathers her grandchildren around her on Sherman Avenue. The house in the left background is on Second Court. The children from left to right are Martha, Mary, Sherry, Jimmy, and Joseph Frederickson. (MFS.)

A. I. and Pincie (Watkins) Rogers are shown here c. 1952. He was a millwright at International Paper Company. They had four children: Houston, Sybil, Bettie, and Verniece. (VRM.)

Carl Millis and Verniece Rogers are standing near the government housing project in Millville. The homes were built when World War II brought so many new families to work at Tyndall Field (now Tyndall Airforce Base) and the Wainwright Shipyard in the St. Andrews section of Panama City. (VRM.)

Pictured are Jack Bazzell holding his son Mark, Lois McNeil Bazzell, Louise Russ, and Billy Whitehurst. These photographs show the "Teen Timers" who remained friends for life after they married and had families. (VRM.)

Shown here are from left to right are Ed and Emmeline (Hutto) Parrish, Verniece and Carl Millis, and their children Carleen and Clark. (VRM.)

On Easter morning 1976, Mrs. Calvin (Virginia) Bruner is shown with her son, Steven. She was a foreman at the Port Authority, retiring in 1991. (SB.)

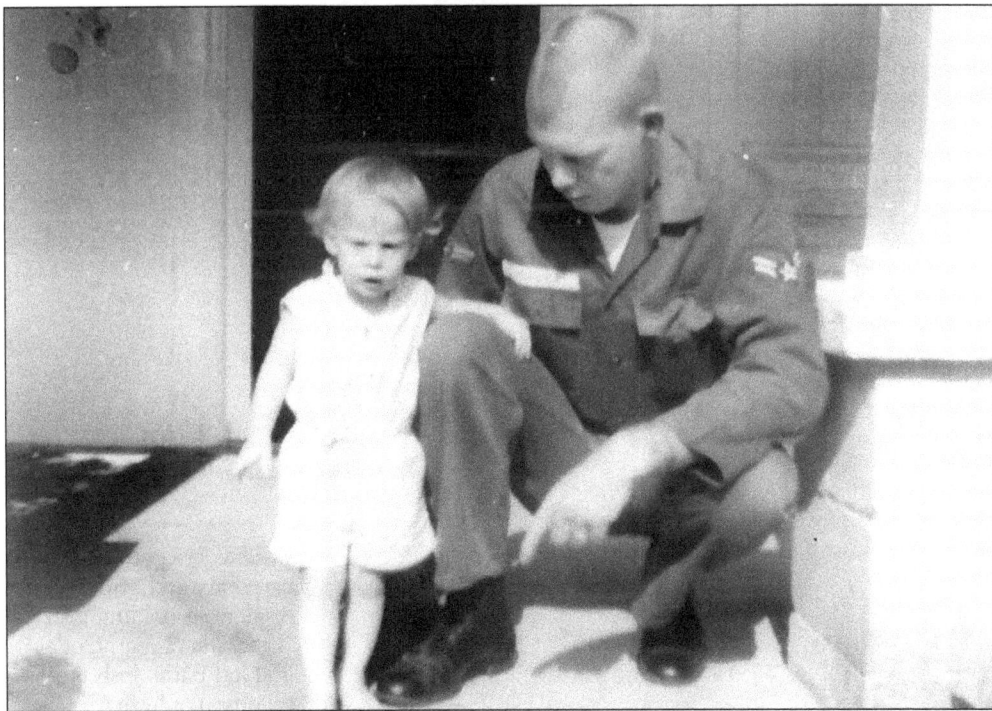

Amanda Bruner is shown with her daddy, Calvin Bruner, who served a hitch in the Air Force. Later he was a professional bull rider in the rodeo. The Bruners lived at 606 Center Avenue. (SB.)

This photograph from a 1948 Christmas card is of Carl and Austine Gray and their daughter, Betty. Carl Gray served seven years as mayor of Panama City from 1948 to 1955. (RC.)

Bill Frederickson, ship carpenter and Millville resident, is holding Josh Batte, son of Joan Corley and Jeff Batte. Josh is a grandson of Jesse (Toby) and Mary Frederickson Corley. (MFS.)

John and Lillian Pratt Anderson are pictured here in the 1940s. They owned the Millville Service Station. Mrs. Anderson's sister, Belle, was the wife of Jasper Jasperson. (JW.)

This is the home of John and Lillian Anderson on Highway 98 East in Millville near Everitt Avenue, which is the dividing line of Millville and the city of Springfield. (JAC.)

LeAnne Robbins, youngest daughter of Richard and Anne Robbins, is shown at her grandparents' home in October 1979. She was eight years old. (DAR.)

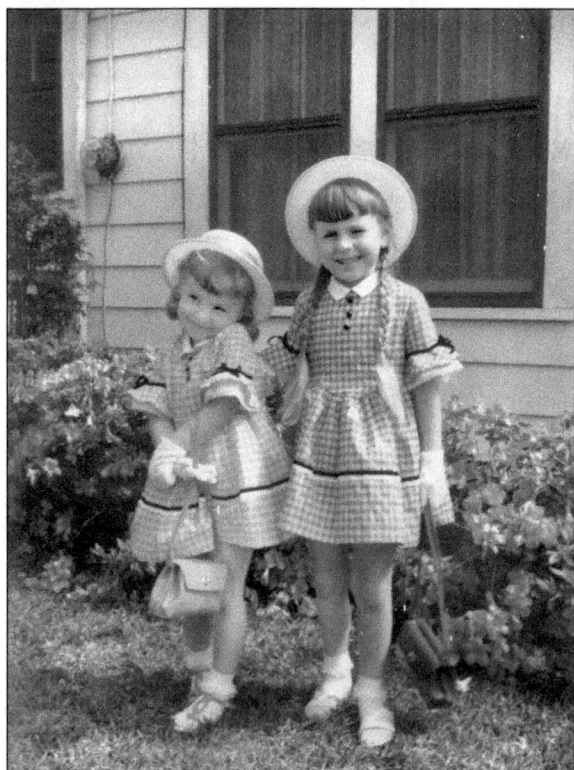

Pamela, left, and Cynthia Robbins, granddaughters of Mr. and Mrs. Johnson, are shown at Easter about 1968. LeAnne, shown above, is their little sister. (DAR.)

Robert C. and Pauline Johnson are pictured here in the 1960s. He worked at International Paper Mill. They were married 63 years. (AJR.)

This is the Johnson home at 204 Kraft Avenue where Ann Johnson grew up. (DAR.)

This gathering includes from left to right (first row) Carl Millis holding his son, Clark; Frances Hill; and Roland Joiner; (second row) Ruby Goff; George Hill Jr.; Stella Hill; George Hill Sr.; Louise ?, holding Carleen Millis; and Lettie Joiner c. 1955. (VRM.)

Sarah Williams Frederickson (Mrs. Bill Frederickson) is shown with her sisters and brothers. From left to right are (first row) John, Sarah (Sadie), Vera, and Katie Lou; (second row) Preston and Ace. (MFS.)

Mr. and Mrs. Ralph Conrad are shown at Immanuel Baptist Homecoming in 1989. Ralph's father was Paul D. Conrad. His uncle, Hiram Conrad, had the oyster bar in downtown Millville. (RC.)

These members of the Gainer family include from left to right Virginia, Bob, James, Josie Mae, and Loran Gainer, shown at 6614 Nadine Road. The photograph was taken in 1983. (GFC.)

The Cotton family members shown here are from left to right are Charles Jr., Gladys, Ira, Percy, Eunice "Mama" Cotton, Eunice Elizabeth, Mary Belle, and Bernice. (CFC.)

Lined up for a picture c. 1942 are from left to right are Charles Christopher Cotton, John Arthur Hutton, Peggy Cotton, Percy Scott Cotton Jr. (in front of Peggy), Dorothy Eunice Cotton, Thelma Eunice Bauler, Eunice Ann Hutton, and Jane Christine Cotton. The annual family reunion brochures are titled "The Cotton Patch." (CFC.)

Three
MILLVILLE SCHOOL

New $20,000.00
High School Building,
Millville, Fla.

This postcard is titled "New $20,000.00 High School Building, Millville, Fla." In the January 18, 1908, *Panama City Pilot*, a writer mentions, "A school presided over by the popular instructor, Prof. Pratt, ably assisted by two other teachers, is an honor to the place." Enrollment in 1908 was 150. This school building later burned. Students then went to Panama City High School. (BCPL.)

This is the Millville Grammar School class of 1918. Mrs. Lewis Scharick (Jewel Pickens Scharick) was the teacher. Identifications of students are not available. (BCPL.)

Shown here is the eighth-grade class at Millville School in 1920. Students included are as follows: Vera Pratt, Alberta Poppell, Lillian Rhodes, Crecia Lynn, Annie Belle Russ, Vogel Rowell, Juliette Anderson, Mary Blitch, Bessie Smith, Bessie Clark, Edna Powell, Herman Cypret, ? Ward, Noah Laird, Bessie Ward, J. V. Jordan, Toby Skinner, James Poston, Johnnie Thomas, Joel Cox, Douglas Barrow, Hulan Bannerman, Harvey Pratt, Harold Marging, George Kockling, George Kimball, Hector Jones, Mary Gray, Clyo Pelham, Eva Brown, and James Lee Skinner. Bertha Henderson was the teacher. (BCPL.)

Bessie Gainey, teacher, stands behind her first-grade class at Millville School in 1928. Students are from left to right (first row) unidentified, Judy Rigell Gaunt, Dorothy Buffalo, ? Clanton, unidentified, Sara Alice Singletary Hallmon, Maggie Mink, Oma Hawkins, unidentified, and Louise Virginia Holmes Kelly; (second row) two unidentified, Dorthea Torgorsen, Hobson Laird, Fred Turner, Vera Lee Warren Jones, Rudolph Pitts, Donnie Hagans (died in 1930), unidentified, Dick Scott, ? Clanton, Don Weeks, Hillman Conant, Ovita Ard, and Esby Davidson. (BCPL.)

This 8th-grade graduating class photograph possibly from the mid-1920s is labeled simply "a Millville class." (BCPL.)

Millville's 8th-grade graduating class is photographed in May 1939. Members were not identified. (BCPL.)

The graduation of the eighth-grade class of 1940–1941 was held in the Millville Assembly of God's first sanctuary across the street from the later, bigger building. Shown from left to right are (first row) Albert Brown, Mary Grace Silcox, Charles Chesnut, Elwin Stubbs, W. C. Cooper, Loudell Kirkland, Rothie Rushing, Myrtle Lowrey, Eugene Boddy, Lillian Lynn, and James Ray Brookins; (second row) Mrs. Chapman (teacher), Principal Mr. Williams, Mrs. Yarbrough (teacher), George McGrannie, Ruth Minshew, Joe ?, Elizabeth Strickland, Gerald Hodsen, Mattie P. Maldin, Sherman Brookins, and Iris Brown; (third row) Donnell Armstrong, Iris Savelle, Betty Lou Lowe, ? Self, Dan Hutchinson, Roger George, Billy Clanton, Betty Sue Knowles, Terry Lane, Eunice Merchant, Hilman Brannon, Virginia Strickland, John Max Hinson, and Inez Hutto; (fourth row) Gene Birch, W. D. Brookins, Betty Jean Arnold, Norma Carl Weaver, Lake Self, Henry Blair, John Hatcher, Mildred Redmon, Montese Marlowe, Herman Godwin, Hubert Kirkland, Louise Davis, Mr. Goddard (teacher), Olan Cannington, Lois ?, Jack Lane, Opal Brackin, and Hazel ?; (fifth row) Jacqueline Sorensen, Walter Williford, Jewel Rayborn, Curtis Marre, Myrtle Pitts, Joyce Holland, Margurite Marlowe, Jeraldine Coatney, Jack Self, James Franklin, Zolema Walker, Mildred Register, Nona Irby, Mamie Sowell, Malissie Walters, Willis York, Louise ?, John Miller, Neamon Hutto, Mary Musgrove, Jack Weeks, Doris Whirley, Charles Anderson, Byron Dunham, Billy Davis, Christelle Peoples, Betty Jean ?, Ralph George, Betty Jean Cox, and Frances Weston. (JSH.)

Millville's third-grade class in 1944 is shown here. From left to right are (first row) Carroll Dees, Russell Phillips, three unidentified, Joan Culbreth, unidentified, Billie Blackwell, and Hazel Mullis; (second row) unidentified, Ramona Parker, Charlotte Campbell, unidentified, Mary Burch, ? Savelle, and two unidentified; (third row) Leonard Goff, Johnny Mack Smith, unidentified, Shirley Teagle, and two unidentified; (fourth row) Jimmy Courtney, two unidentified, George Hicks, and Ms. Gillis (teacher). (RP.)

This class had two snapshots; in the first, the dog was walking around in front, and the children were apparently gesturing at him. So he just lay down and went to sleep. Elizabeth Phillips is on the second row, fourth from left. No other identifications are available. (VRM.)

Shown here is the faculty of Millville School in the 1940s. The pastor's wife, Rose Ferrell, remembers that in the early 1940s teachers were paid $3 per day. When the Wainwright Shipyard opened in St. Andrews and was paying $1 per hour, many teachers quit and went to work out there. The Millville School principal called on Mrs. Ferrell to fill in as a teacher. Among the teachers shown here are, from left to right, (seated incudes) Kate Hubbard (left) and Marcile Leiter (second from left); (back row includes) Principal M. M. Mashburn (Back row center), Mr. Camp (back row, right center), and Bessie Gainey. (BCPL.)

The 1947–1948 graduation ceremonies for Millville School were held in the First Assembly of God sanctuary. Seated on the first row, from left to right, are Mr. Camp, Gladys Chapman, Mr. Wyatt, Ada Leiter, M. M. Mashburn and unidentified. (BCPL.)

58

The only identification provided for this fifth-grade class picture from Russell Phillips' photograph collection is of Mrs. Allen, the teacher, located in the left of the back row. This class may have graduated 8th grade *c.* 1949. (RP.)

Ruth T. Sorensen taught fourth, fifth, and sixth grades at Millville School from 1936 to 1946. She also was the first full-time librarian between 1943 and 1945. (BCPL.)

A student snapped this photograph of two favorite teachers in 1951. The sixth-grade teacher, Marcile Leiter, is on the left, and Ruth Collins, the school librarian, is on the right. (DAR.)

COMPLIMENTS OF "THE BAY LINE"

Mrs. Crawford's fifth-grade class trip on the Bay Line was a high point of the school year. The children were taken by automobile to Youngstown, where they got on the train. A class member was able to identify some of those pictured. Included from left to right are (first row) Ethel Swindell, Joyce Tyre, Rita Conrad, and five unidentified; (second row) unidentified, ? George, unidentified, R. L. Emanuel, and unidentified; (third row) Mrs. Conrad, Donna Youngblood, ? George, Nell ?, five unidentified, Yvonne Gortman, three unidentified, James Warren, two unidentified, Sue ?, ? George, Ann Price, Sula Turner, three unidentified, and Mrs. Wells (substitute teacher). (DYM.)

This photograph was taken on Mrs. Hubbard's third-grade class trip in 1949, a train ride from Youngstown to Panama City. Some of the students are Bill Gainey (front row, far left), Joanne Davis (second row, far left), and Carol McKinney (third row, far left). (MFS.)

This photograph of a class trip on the Bay Line is from Ann Johnson's collection. (DAR.)

Miss. Tew's second-grade class is shown in 1946. Martha Frederickson Suggs is in the background, in the back row next to the teacher. Ernestine Williams is in front at left. (MFS.)

Another view of Miss Tew's second-grade class, now lined up for their picture in 1946, shows, from left to right (first row) three unidentified, Bobby Williams, unidentified, Bill Gainey, unidentified, Jimmy Paulk, and Miss. Tew; (second row) five unidentified, Howard ?, and unidentified; (third row) five unidentified, Ernestine Williams, and two unidentified; (fourth row) two unidentified, Martha Frederickson, and seven unidentified. (MFS.)

This photograph shows Marcile Leiter's sixth graders in 1951. (DAR.)

Shown here are the girls in Miss. Leiter's sixth-grade class. Among them are Jane Dawsen (back row, far left), Wanda Barnes (back row, third from left), and Angeline Bedsole (back row, far right). (DAR.)

Here is another view of Millville Elementary School on East Avenue. The photograph was probably taken in the 1940s. The building burned in 1975 during Christmas vacation. (BCPL.)

Millville School
Grade 5
1948 - 1949

This is the class picture of the Millville fifth grade of 1948–1949. From left to right and top to bottom are Elizabeth Phillips (first row, third from left), Linda Huges (second row, second from the left); Carolyn Ameson (third row, far left); Charles Smith (third row, second from left); Rosa Lea Brown (third row, third from left); Joyce McDaniel (fourth row, fourth from left); and Abbie Lynn Ingram (fifth row, fourth from left). (RP.)

This is the Millville fourth-grade class in 1948–1949. From left to right and top to bottom are (first row) Miss Leiter, three unidentified, Angeline Bedsole, and unidentified; (second row) Edward Yerby, Catherine Burkett, unidentified, and Ann Johnson; (third row) Shannan Wester, Charles ?, unidentified, Allan Miller, Sue Lisenby, and Jack Wright; (fourth row) Harold Brookins, Helen Fay Walters, unidentified, Barbara Gilbert, James Killingsworth, and Joy ?; (fifth row) Sandra Clark, Audrey ?, Janie Dawsell, two unidentified, and Wayne Spikes; (sixth row) Nell Bozeman, two unidentified, Larry Redmon, and unidentified. (DAR.)

Millville's grade five in 1949–1950 included, from left to right and top to bottom, (first row) Miss Moore, unidentified, Joy ?, Jimmy Gray, Mary Brannon, unidentified, Ann Johnson, James Adkinson, and Catherine Burkett; (second row) unidentified, Wanda Barnes, two unidentified, Penny ?, and Joe Dixon; (third row) Jane ?, Royal Murphy, two unidentified, Janice Musgrove, Robert Richardson, Sue Barnes, and two unidentified; (fourth row) Charles Cunningham, Harold Brookins, Jack Wright, Shannon Wester, unidentified, Thomas Holman, unidentified, and Charles ?. (DAR.)

This is the 1947 Millville girls' basketball team. Shown here from left to right are (first row) ? Savelle, R. Parker, unidentified, Joan Culbreth, Betty Sue Whirley, Mary Ingram, and unidentified; (second row) Betty Roughton, Ann Casey, Virginia Richardson, J. Jenkins, J. Stanifer, Jeannine George, two unidentified, and Imogene Morris; (third row) Blondell Blankenship, M. Rowell, unidentified, Olive Jean Owens, Charlotte Campbell, Gloria King, Shirley Teagle, Doris Lee, and unidentified. (BCPL.)

The boys' basketball team c. 1948 includes from left to right (first row) ? Strickland, Billy Wicker, Elzie Bass, James Morris, Grover Hutto, Dayton Kent, and Franklin Whitehurst; (second row) M. M. Mashburn, Bobby Roughton, Bill O'Neal, Johnny Bass, Donald Davis, Jimmy Courtney, and Coach White. (BCPL.)

Hazel Cooper's Girl Scout troop had a dance that required the girls to have an escort c. 1949. Included from left to right are (first row) Dalton Cooper, three unidentified, Arthur Pratt, Donna Youngblood, Betty Guy Cooper, Joyce Tyre, Barbara Blue, Pearl McLemore, unidentified, and Billy Blue; (second row) three unidentified, Joyce Teagle, unidentified, Nanette Whitehurst, three unidentified, and Carolyn Hicks; (third row) three unidentified, Mrs. Blue, two unidentified, Mrs. Teagle, two unidentified, and Shirley Teagle. No other names are known.

Fifth-grader Donna Youngblood was escorted by Arthur Pratt to the Girl Scout dance. (DYM.)

During the 1948–1949 school year, a Brownie group dance was held at the Panama City Civic Center. Martha Frederickson is on the front row at right. (MFS.)

Martha Frederickson is pictured here as she was ready to go to the dance. (MFS.)

Mr. Basil Moore (third row, center) was principal of Millville Elementary School when this Safety Patrol photograph was made in 1959. Clark Millis is on the first row, third from left; Tommy Tiller is fifth from left on the second row, and ? Ramer is on the right in the second row. (VRM.)

A Millville Elementary School class poses on the steps in the 1940s. Individual identifications are not available. (VRM.)

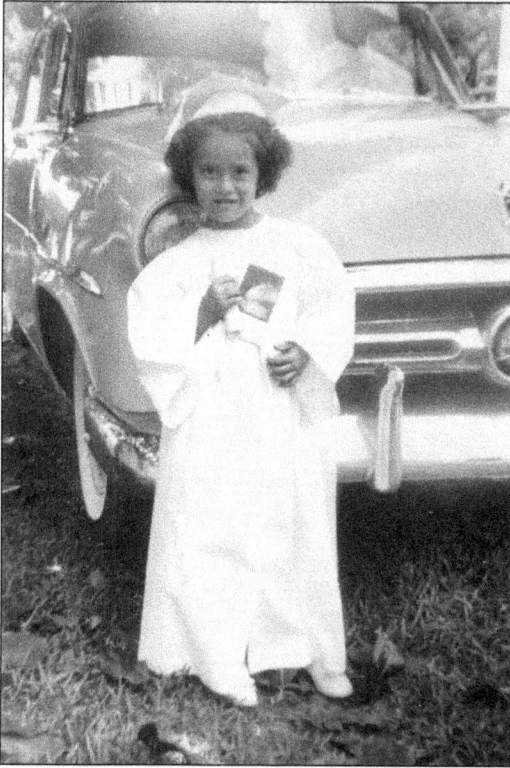

Donna Pratt was sick and did not attend graduation ceremonies at Mrs. Amanda Parker's kindergarten in 1953, but she still got her picture taken. (DPH.)

This is the graduation photograph of Amanda Parker's kindergarten pupils in 1953. Mrs. Parker is to the right of the third row. (DPH.)

Shown here is the 1959–1960 graduation ceremony of the Bo-Peep Kindergarten. Carleen Millis is 10th from left (right under the "B"). (VRM.)

Amanda Parker, kindergarten director, stands behind Kathryn Hanline (daughter of JoAnne Silcox Andrews), a 1959 graduate. (RP.)

At Millville Elementary School, Betty Jett, in a pilgrim costume, leads her kindergarten class in the annual kindergarten Thanksgiving pageant. Teacher's aide JoAnne Meeks, right background, is dressed as a Native American maiden. (BCPL.)

These children in Mrs. Jett's kindergarten class are portraying the pilgrims's Thanksgiving feast.

Four
THE CHURCHES

Pictured is the Immanuel Baptist Church in Millville. One local history indicates that the first church in Millville was the St. James African Methodist Church, established in 1900. A mission of the St. Andrews Baptist Church was established at Millville on August 27, 1900, with 17 charter members. This group became Immanuel Baptist Church, erecting its first building in 1902. The building shown here came later in the development of the church. (BCPL.)

This photograph was made while Millville Assembly of God "was still in the small old church," according to Rose Ferrell. Shown are members of the choir, with Pastor Harvey D. Ferrell and his wife, Rose, holding her piano accordion, which she always played in the services. (RF.)

Pastor Ferrell is standing between two other dads holding their babies with a group of the children at Millville Assembly. This photograph was made in the small old church probably in 1944. (RF.)

Pastor Harvey and Rose Ferrell are shown here as they did their 30-minute radio program Monday through Friday and one-hour program on Sunday. It was the first local church radio program on Panama City radio, and it continued for about five years during the 1940s. (RF.)

Some of the leaders and workers in Millville Assembly are shown with Reverend Ferrell, back row, third from the left. The church was beginning to grow and had over 400 people in Sunday school that day c. 1944. (RF.)

Rev. Adolph Bedsole, pastor of Immanuel Baptist Church in Millville, is shown with the kindergarten graduating class in May 1965. Pictured here from left to right are (first row) Renee Fulford, Linda Conrad, Sherrie Hood, Rebekah Mioller, Donna Hardy, Nancy Clark, and Julianne King; (second row) Reverend Bedsole, Tommy Matthew, Ricky Harvey, Mark Cutshaw, Scott Raffield, James Clewis, and Ruth Conrad. (IBC.)

Members of the Immanuel Baptist Singles Training Union Class are shown in 1948. Pictured here from left to right are (first row) Hazel Devane McCall, Virginia Strickland Stark, Helen Spikes Waters, Nell Harmon, Merial Pitts Wilkerson, Mildred Redmon Clark, Bernice Sloan Carter, and Ellen Money; (second row) Hubert Kirkland, James Sanders, John Clark, Frank Glass, Limon McCall, Johnny Nelson, Wade Waters, and Wallace Fleming. (IBC.)

This photograph was made on groundbreaking day, August 1, 1954, for the new educational building of Immanuel Baptist Church. Rev. Adolph Bedsole, pastor of the church, is in the first row at left. (IBC.)

The Men's Bible Class of the Baptist church posed for this photograph, taken by L. W. Masker of St. Andrews, in 1926. Included here are J. R. Thompson, J. H. Daffin, Frank Wester, A. M. Lewis, R. H. Gray, A. J. Pellum, Lee Cotton, D. D. Laird, ? Weeks, D. F. Davis, Will Lash, Dr. ? Adams, A. I. Singletary, ? Stewart, and ? Smith. Note the stained-glass windows on the church building. (IBC.)

Clark and Carleen Millis are shown outside the Trinity Methodist Church c. 1958. The Methodist church was established in Millville in 1903. (VRM.)

The choir of Trinity United Methodist Church is shown at Christmas time c. 1980. From left to right are David Carter, Travis Scott, Wayne McLead, Thomas Harrison, Don McCormick, Kenny Tiller, unidentified, Jim Pugh, JoAnn Pugh, unidentified, JoAnn Rushing, unidentified, Tilde Harrison, Hazel Bryan, Janet Carter, Margaret Scott (pianist), Mary Tiller, Mary Nell Harrison, Sandra Scott, Arlene Devereux, and two unidentified people. Director Pat McCormick is in front. (BCPL.)

The congregation is shown gathering outside the church at Trinity United Methodist Church on Third Street in Millville c. 1958. (VRM.)

Shown here is the Millville Advent Christian Church, which was established in 1905.

This photograph is of two Millville Assembly Sunday school classes in the 1940s with one of the teachers, Gladys Moses, standing in the back. (RF.)

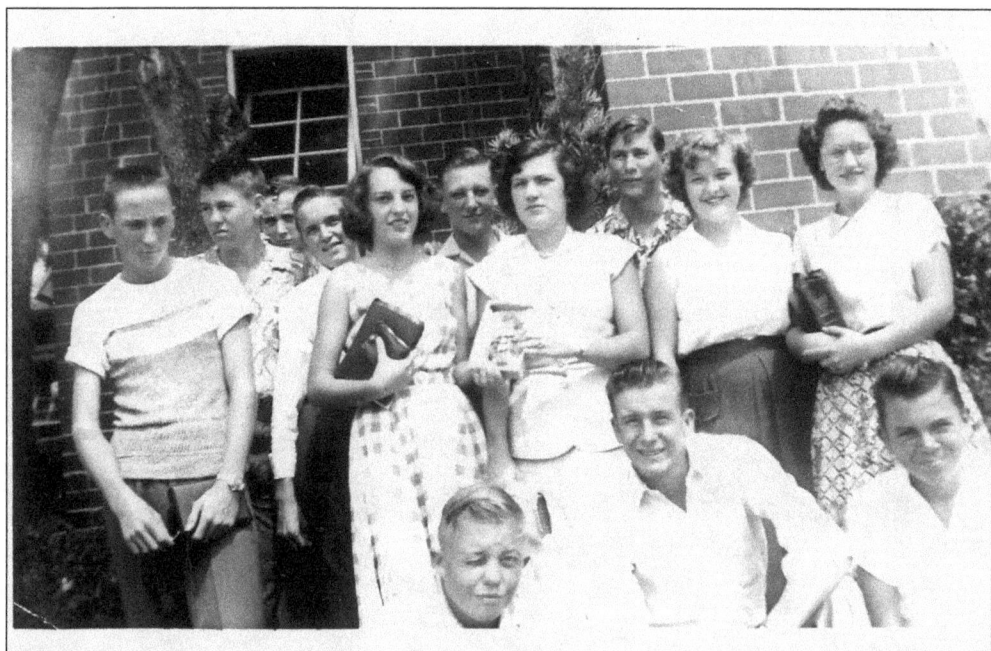

These smiling young people are at the Millville Assembly of God, probably in the mid-1950s. (VRM.)

Drs. David and Vernette Rosier, shown here, are pastors of Fellowship of Praise Church, and Dr. Vernette Rosier is also principal of Fellowship Christian Academy. The church on Third Street in Millville previously served Millville Assembly of God and, later, Calvary Cathedral. (FA.)

This church building, formerly the Millville Assembly of God, now is the home of Fellowship Christian Academy and Church. (AC.)

Eunice Lavonia Scott Cotton is shown in this portrait from the Cotton family collection. Mrs. Cotton is noted in the Immanuel Baptist Church history: "In 1921, Mrs. Eunice Cotton and her family came. Some of her family had already united with the church. So many good things did Mrs. Cotton accomplish in the succeeding 40 years that her record deserves a eulogy." It is reported that "all the visiting ministers stayed at Mama Cottons." (Information IBC; photograph CFC.)

Brown and Lois Spiva owned the Gospel Book and Gift Shop on Highway 98 in Millville for many years. Lois continued to manage the business after Brown's death. The store is used by Sunday school teachers and other church leaders for Bibles and learning materials, and it also provides small appliance repair service. (LS.)

Five

MILLVILLE
AT WORK AND PLAY

Hank Williams sometimes showed up at local businesses with his band. Here he is shown at R. H. Gray's grocery store on Third Street in Millville. Included here in the front row from left to right are Hank Williams, Carl Gray, Becky Barfield, Red Savine, and Pee Wee King. Austine Gray is in the second row on the left. (GG.)

More than 100 of Millville's men served in World War I. Company M, 1st Florida Infantry, National Guard, was formed April 12, 1917, six days after Pres. Woodrow Wilson's declaration of war. F. Marion Turner, superintendent of the lumber company, was the captain; Malle Martin, bookkeeper, was first lieutenant; and Royall DeWatts, saw filer, was second lieutenant, according to Harold Bell in *Glimpses of the Panhandle*. Fitzhugh Lee Cotton, shown above right in uniform during World War I, was a member of the company who served in Europe. James Hinson Harrison, shown standing above left, served in the army also. In the photograph below, citizen-soldiers in Company M line up for service. John Wesley Powell Sr. is third from left. (Above left and below BCPL, right CFC.)

Many Tyndall servicemen attended church in Millville. This is Major Emery and his wife and daughter, who all went to Millville Assembly while stationed at Tyndall Field. (RF.)

Jasper and Belle Jasperson are shown in front of their house in Millville with their son, Glenn, during World War II. (JW.)

Bob and Odeal Gainer are shown at 3002 East Third Street in the 1940s. (GFC.)

Odeal Gainer is seated with her children, Gerald and Ann, outside the USO building at the foot of Harrison Avenue during World War II. (GFC.)

When Bob Gainer went away to war, Odeal vowed not to cut her son's hair until her husband returned safely. This photograph shows Gerald with shoulder-length hair, just before his father came home. (GFC.)

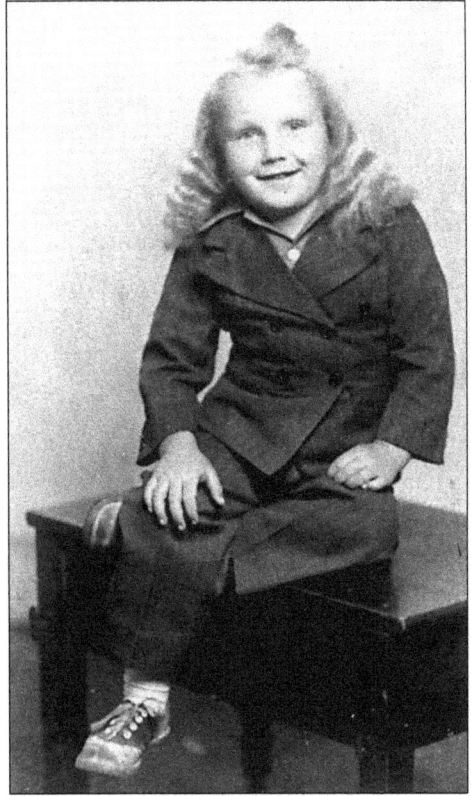

This 1946 photograph shows Gerald, who got a short haircut as soon as his father returned home safely. (GFC.)

This group of Millville servicemen includes from left to right: (top row) Carl Carter (photographed June 27, 1944); Carl Caswell Jr., who married Oveal Carter while in the service; and Cleatous Carter, who served in the Fifth Army in Germany from 1942 to 1947; (bottom row) Jesse (Toby) Corley and his son, Jesse, who followed his father into the navy; U.S. Marine James Gainer; and Benjamin Francis Cotton of the Army Air Corps, who was killed during flight training. (Top row and bottom middle images GFC, bottom left MFS, bottom right CFC.)

Benjamin Francis Cotton is shown here while serving as a flight training student. He was killed in a plane crash during training. (CFC.)

Pictured in front of the Cotton's Millville home in 1943, from left to right, are Mary Belle, Gladys Louise, Eunice Lavonia, Ira Melinda, and Eunice Elizabeth Cotton with the soldier who accompanied the body of Benjamin Francis home. (CFC.)

H. Ralph Conrad and his wife, Delia Anderson Conrad, are shown during World War II. They have one daughter, Beverly. (RC.)

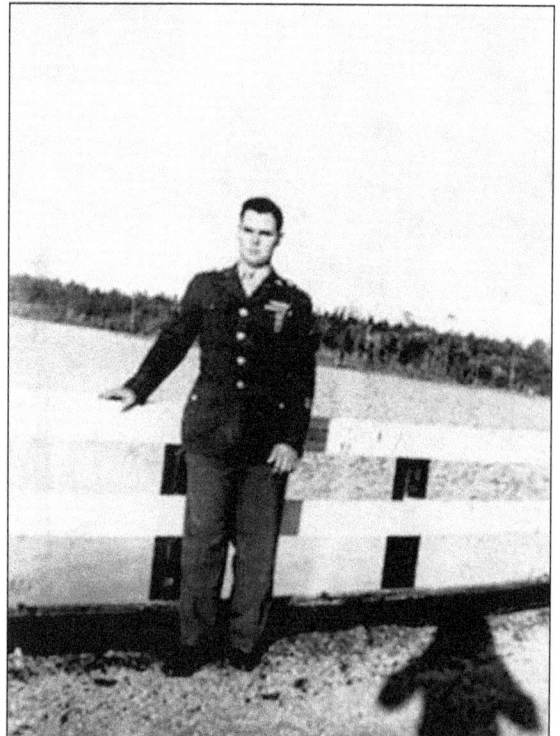

Thomas Dallas Harrison is pictured in World War II uniform. He married Mary Nell Bardon, and they had two daughters, Cynthia and Janet. He and his father, James, owned Harrison Mercantile in downtown Millville. In the early 1970s, he became a dispatcher with the fire station, serving until the advent of 911 service. The Harrison home is at 2200 Third Street. (JHC.)

Young people seemed to be attracted to cars and liked to sit on them. Frank Stricklen, son of Alex Stricklen and Bessie Lee Smith Stricklen, is shown with his wife's sister, Pat Trayler. The young boy on the car is Joe Tom Hall, brother of Frank's wife, Doris Trayler Stricklen. (DAR.)

Shown here in the Millville cemetery are Joe Frederickson and his sisters, Martha and Mary, at the time of the death of their great-grandmother, Mary Theresa Sconiers, in 1949. (MFS.)

This photograph of John Phillips as a boy was taken about 1910. He is the father of Russell and Elizabeth Phillips. (R.P.)

Shown in a matching photograph is John's wife, Gussie, as a young girl probably about 1920. (R.P.)

Harold Jasperson Jr., at about age two, watches intently as his uncle, J. E., works on the back end of a car c. 1940. (HJ.)

Steven Bruner seems to be saying, "When it's hot summertime, all you can do is dive into that wading pool." (SB.)

Russell Phillips makes friends with some chickens in the 1940s. (RP.)

A smiling Harold Jasperson appears to be dressed for church. When he grew up, he was employed as a welder at International Paper Company. (DPH.)

Randall H. Gray, six, and his brother
Carl, eight, are shown in 1922. The boys
and their brother John (not pictured)
were the sons of R. H. Gray, who operated
the general store at Center Avenue and
Third Street in Millville. The three sons
all helped out at the store. As an adult,
Carl had a daily radio news program,
served several terms in the Florida
Legislature, and also served as mayor of
Panama City. (BCPL.)

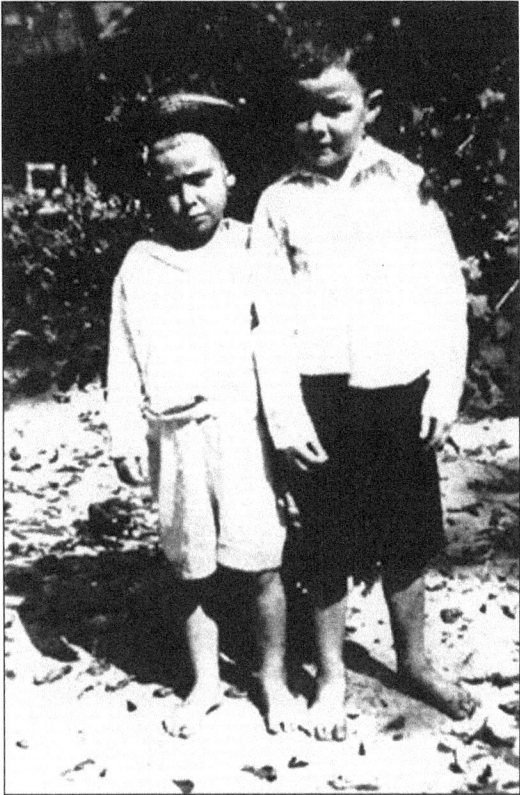

Roy and Rita Conrad, children of Hiram and Mamie
Ruth Conrad, enjoy a ride in their goat cart on
August 8, 1942. (RC.)

The Teen Timers were a group of girls who joined together into a social club while in the seventh grade at Millville Grammar School in 1947. The softball team included in 1947, from left to right, (first row) Bobbie Jean Brookins Tew, Joann Silcox Andrews, Lois McNiel Bazzell, Betty Bryant Pitts, Lenoma "Shorty" Reese Daugherty, and Jean Lee Bozeman; (second row) Nina Lee White Lecompt, Doris Lee Odum, Betty Sue Hammonds Moses, Patsy Musgrove Donaldson, Jerry Hartzog Bozeman, and Ann Stanley (now deceased). (VRM.)

The Teen Timers's 15th anniversary in 1952 included, from left to right, Alice Scott White, Evon Blount Raffield, Verniece Rogers Millis, Ann Walls Cook, Julia Vickers Hagler, Blondell Blankenship Wright, Betty Hammonds Brown Moses, and Bobbie Brookins Tew. (VRM.)

Leaning on a fence from left to right are Freddie Knowler, Jo Anne Silcox, Doug Knowler, Charles Silcox, and Betty Sue Knowler.

The Teen Timers who gathered for the 54th annual reunion dinner were from left to right (first row) Ann Walls Cook, Lois Bazzell, Bobbie Tew, Verniece Millis, Shorty Daugherty, and Evon Raffield; (second row) Joann Andrews, Betty Green, Louise Whitehurst, Ruth Miller, Louise Hicks, and Alice White; (third row) Billie Rosser, Betty Pitts, Betty Jean Barrett, Betty Moses, Shirley Burke, Betty Jo Anderson, Betty Jean Bowden, Blondell Wright, Ann Couchagen, and June Johnson. (VRM.)

Enjoying a Kathy Hanline's sixth birthday party are from left to right Joanne Bozeman Ray, Kathy Keebler, Mary Jo Hanline, Ken Brock, Kathy Hanline, JoAnne Whitaker, and Sue Whitaker. (KH.)

Verniece Millis, back left, and Evon Raffield, back right, are shown with their Brownie troop crossing over the bridge to become Girl Scouts. Brownie Carleen Millis is at left. (VRM.)

M. J. "Doc" Daffin was born in Millville in 1902 and served as Bay County's eighth sheriff. He became sheriff in 1952 and served five four-year terms and one two-year term. During his career, he was once removed from office by the Florida governor and immediately voted back into office in the next regular election. In January 1971, Daffin died from a stroke while in office. (BCPL.)

Sheriff M. J. 'Doc' Daffin

Two men are shown in retirement ceremonies at International Paper Company on July 1, 1977. Clyde Jones, left holding certificate, was retiring after 33 years at the mill; Robert C. Johnson, right holding certificate, was retiring after 31 years. The two mill officials are not identified. (DAR.)

This is a Cotton family Halloween party c. 1951. The reader is invited to identify the partygoers if possible. (CFC.)

Family reunions are always fun, especially when the Cotton family gets together. In 1957, "Cotton Patch" members were, from left to right, Eunice Ann Hutton, Ira Joe Greene, Dorothy Eunice Cotton, Charles Daniel King, Barbara Louise Cotton, Anita Paige Bauler, Marcia Louise King, Ira Janine King, Bernice Phillip Cotton, Eunice "Mama" Cotton, Ethel Eunice Greene, Thelma Eunice Bauler, Martha Frances Cotton, Marjorie Grace Peggy Cotton, and Virginia Gayle Cotton. (CFC.)

A picnic at Bob George Park, which used to be located on East Avenue near Millville School, was a tradition with the Rogers family. A. I. Rogers, who loved picnics, is seated at left; George Hill is standing in the background; and Carl Millis is seated at right. (VRM.)

Mr. and Mrs. Bill Frederickson are shown at a birthday celebration in the 1960s. (MFS.)

Carl and Gladys Carter are pictured with their cow at their home at 3012 East Third Street in Millville. (GFC.)

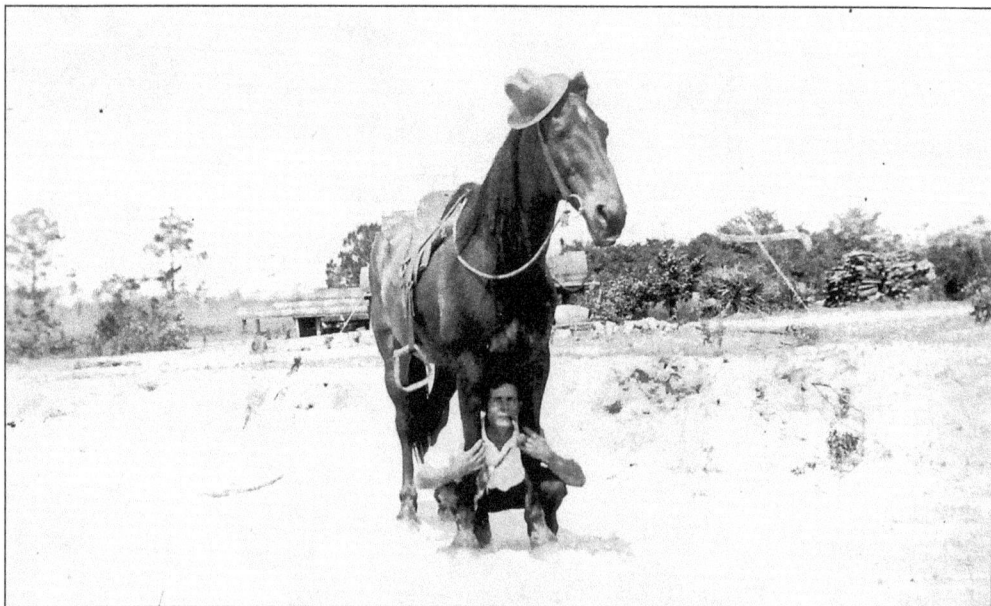

Donny Byrd, brother of Mary Youngblood, poses with his horse, probably in the late 1930s or early 1940s. (DYM.)

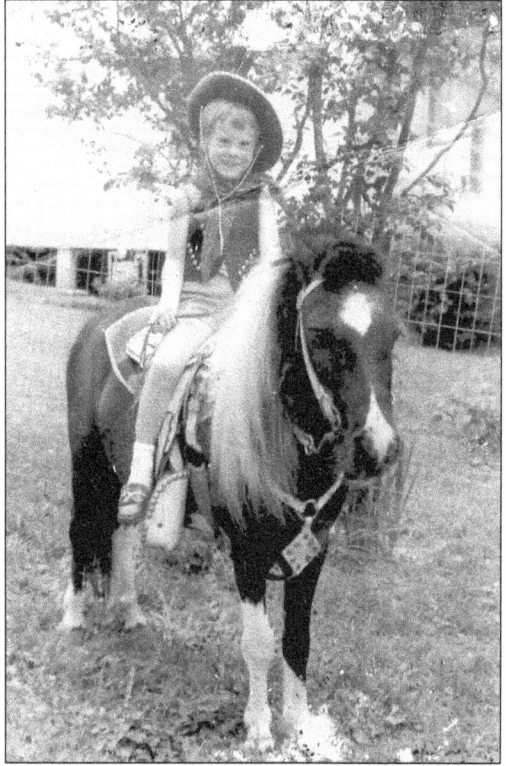

Amanda Bruner looks sharp in her cowgirl outfit riding her pony in the summer of 1971. (SB.)

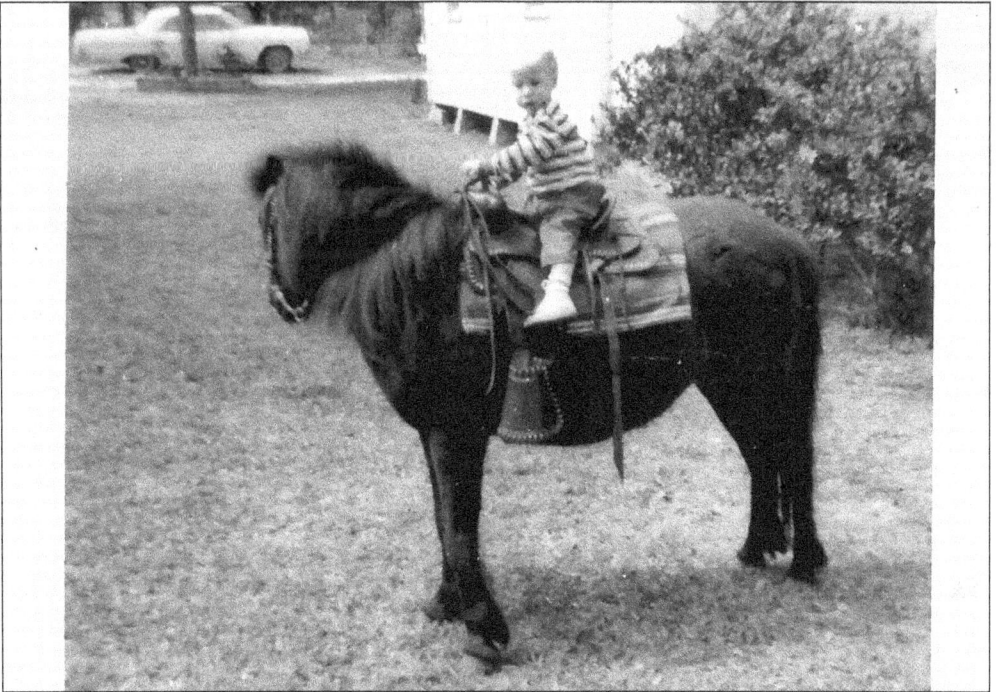

Amanda's little brother, Steven, is also a pony rider, even though his feet don't reach the stirrups. This picture was taken in the summer of 1972. (SB.)

Paul D. ("Samson") Conrad, billed as the "strongest boy in the South," holds A. Crawford Mosley one-handed over his head at Panama City Beach. Conrad's feats appeared in *Ripley's Believe It or Not* at least four times. One of his records still stands: he climbed the Washington Monument carrying a man on his shoulders in less than 17 minutes. (RC.)

Here Paul Conrad holds boards through which he has driven nails with his hands. He was listed four times in *Ripley's Believe It or Not*. Conrad owned a gym in Millville, later moving it to Panama City. (RC.)

This is the Millville Peewees football team c. 1970. Teams from every school participate in the Gulf Coast Midget League. The annual Snapper Bowl is the big event of the league. Harold M. Creel, president of the league in 2005, has been active in the organization since 1961. (BCPL.)

Here are the Millville Tiny Mites. (BCPL.)

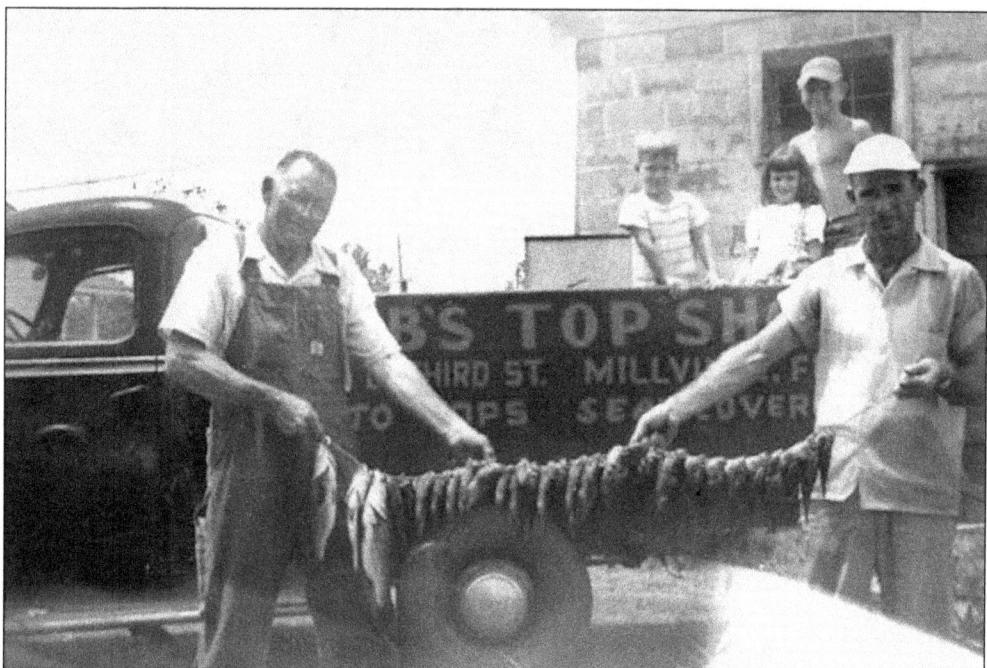

Carl Carter and Bob Gainer lift a fine string of fish as Marvin Caswell, Ann Gainer, and Gerald Gainer look on. They are in front of Bob's Top Shop truck at 3012 East Third Street in Millville. (GFC.)

A Jasperson family group is shown with their catch after a successful fishing trip. (HJ.)

Percy Cotton is pictured here with a Warsaw grouper after a deep-sea fishing trip, c. 1965. (CFC.)

Charlie Cotton won the trophy for this grouper in a Captain Anderson Fishing Tournament in 1972. The avid fisherman didn't let diabetes keep him from fishing. (CFC.)

Boat racing was a very popular sport in the Southeast. These Bay County racing teams are on the way to boat races in Florala, Alabama, in the late 1940s. (CFC.)

This race was taking place on Watson Bayou c. 1945. Note the "Cotton's Grocery" on the side of the boat, which was owned by the Cotton brothers—Bernice, Charlie, and Percy. (CFC.)

The Cotton family is on an egg hunt at Easter 1954. (CFC.)

In this photograph, Percy Cotton is racing *Cotton Grocery* on Watson Bayou c. 1945. (CFC.)

Ann Johnson, daughter of R. C. and Pauline Strickland Johnson, is shown exercising her short hair pointers, Danny Boy and Trouble, in 1956. Pointers were used a lot in the panhandle of Florida for hunting quail. Ann and her dogs took many walks around Millville during the 1950s. Ann's father, known as "Peck," worked at the paper mill. (DAR.)

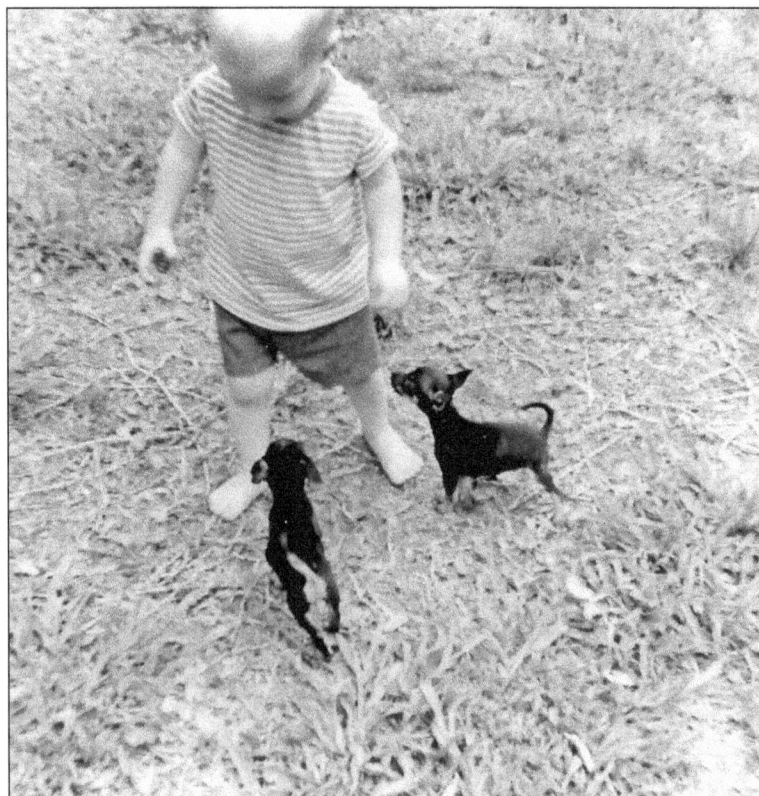

Steven Bruner, about three years old, is seen playing with two Chihuahuas. (SB.)

The occasion of this photograph was a wedding shower for Donna Youngblood, who was engaged to marry Lee Mattern. Shown from left to right are Donna's mother, Mary Youngblood; Ola McKinnan; Ardelia Brown; Maggy Talley; Donna Youngblood; Myrtle Shoemaker; Mrs. A. L. Bunche; and Mrs. Coy Owens. (DYM.)

This is a group of grandchildren and great-grandchildren of Anna Lou (Youngblood) Spurlock at 138 Kraft Avenue c. 1964. From left to right are Denise Armstrong, unidentified, Diane Helms, Angela Armstrong, Wilbur Armstrong, Byrd Youngblood, Steven Youngblood, Monica Mattern, Mary Vickie Mattern, and James Youngblood. (DYM.)

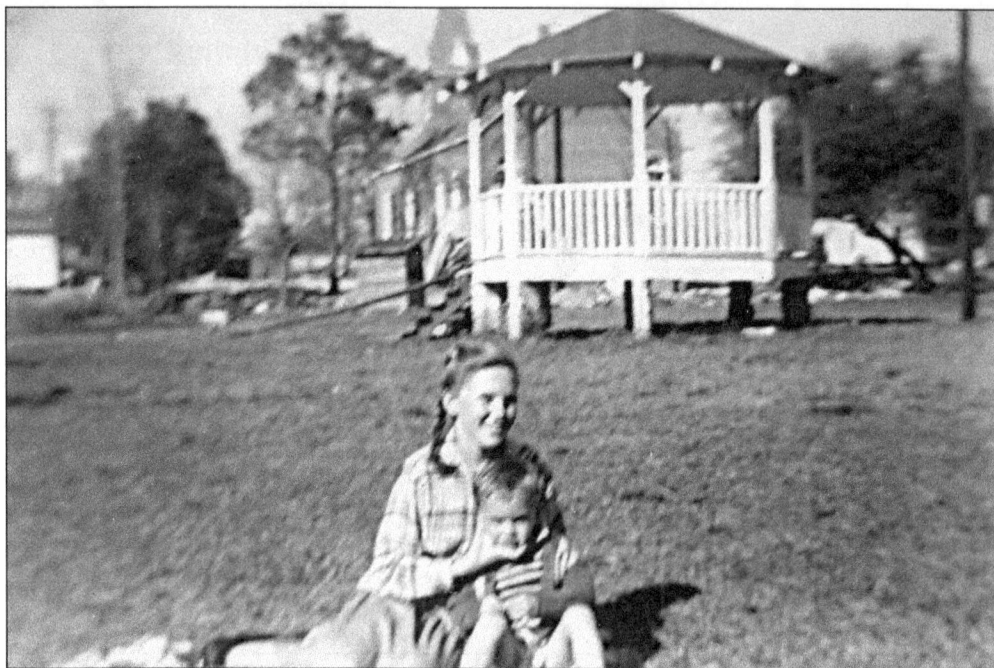

Joanne Silcox Andrews and Jimmy Musgrove enjoy the outdoors in this photograph made at Kidd Harris Park in Millville. Most everybody played outside, finding plenty of ways to play and not wanting to stay indoors or underfoot. Kidd Harris Park was a great place to play stickball and other outdoor games. The bandstand was used for political rallies and musical concerts. Fish fries and picnics were held in the park, which is still in use. Television didn't appear in the local area until 1953, and everyone didn't get a TV set right away even then. (KH.)

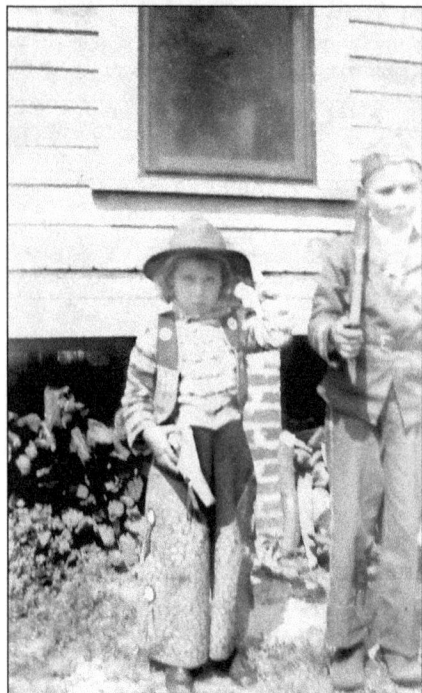

Another favorite outdoor pastime was playing cowboys, as Donna and Dickie Youngblood are doing in this photograph. (DYM.)

If nothing else, there was always softball. Parents had to decide if they wanted a nice lawn or a play yard for the kids. Gerri Paulk gets ready to hit as Ann Johnson pitches the ball. (DAR.)

Sitting on a fence are three cowboys, dressed up, armed and dangerous—Charles Silcox (left), Doug Knowles (center), and Phil Silcox. (KH.)

John and Gussie Phillips are holding their grandson, Charles, in 1961. (RP.)

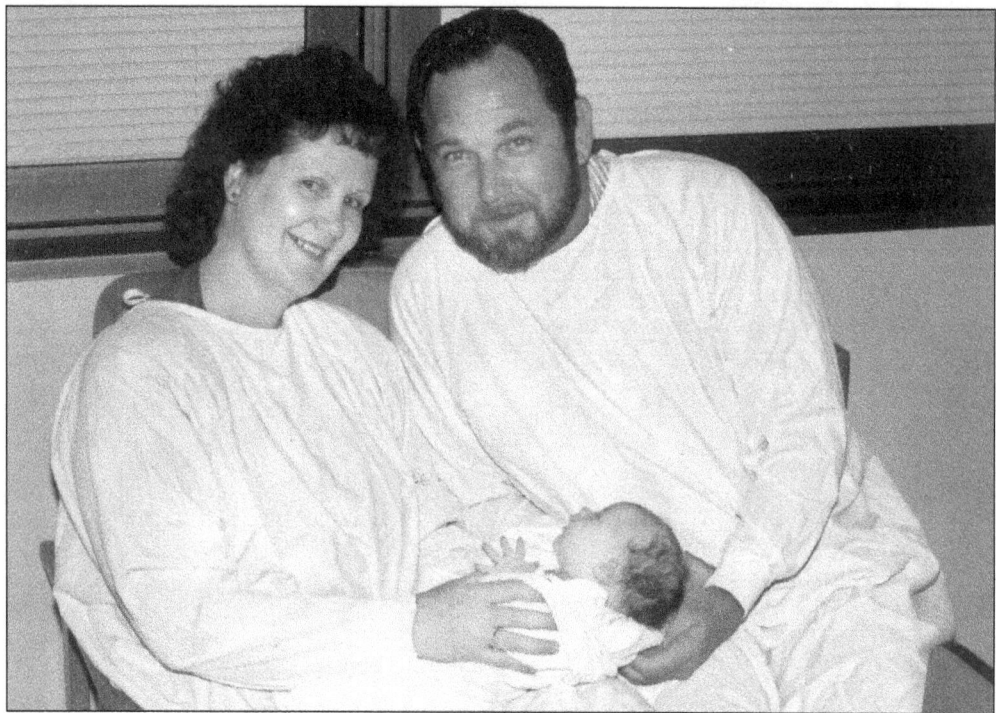

Sharon and Ralph Conrad, shown here on May 2, 1990, are holding their newborn granddaughter, Cassidy Lane, who is the daughter of Carolyn and Ray Webb. (RC.)

These toddlers are in an album of the Bill Frederickson family. From left to right are (first row) Billy Blackwell, Catherine Burkett, and Martha Frederickson; (second row) Jerry Strickland, and Joe Frederickson, holding a duck his father made. (MFS.)

The senior citizen center at Daffin Park Clubhouse in Millville is the scene of this family gathering. From left to right are (first row) Katie Lou Hartzog, Sarah (Sadie) Frederickson, Vera Hartzog, and John Williams; (second row) Preston Williams, Preacher Ace Williams, and Clayton Williams. (MFS.)

Oveal Carter is ready for a Millville Elementary School program. (GFC.)

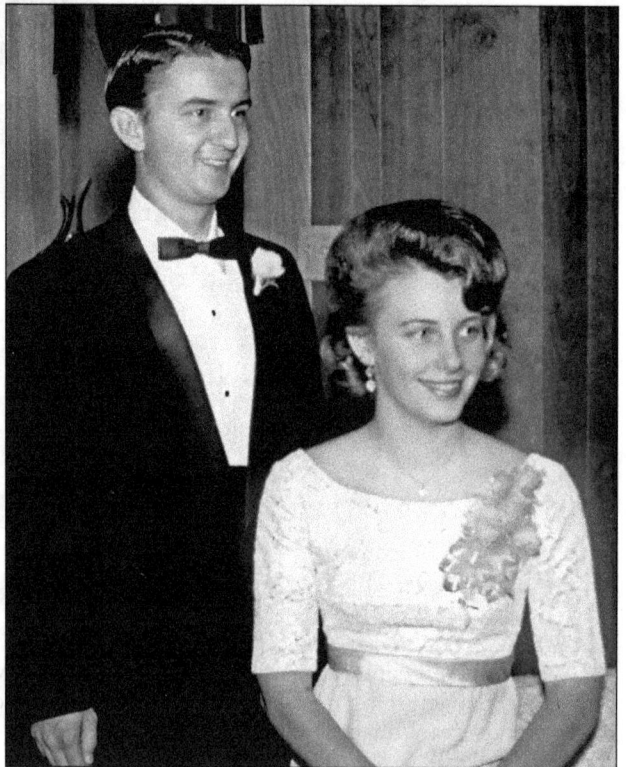

Shown here in 1966 are Billy Fussell and Glenda Gainer. They both became teachers in the Bay County system, and they later married. (GFC.)

116

This is the Jitney Jungle Store, which was opened by L. D. Lewis in Millville as "Panama City, Florida Number 2" in 1948 and served the east side for many years. It later became the Sunshine Market, and as the business expanded, Lewis became known as Sunshine Lewis and had stores in several states. (LJB.)

A newspaper writer stated in the *Panama City News Herald*: "The photographer catches one of the high points of L. D. Lewis's career as a Jitney Jungle operator. L. M. Walker, contractor for the Number 2 store cuts the ribbon to officially open the tour of the new store as Lewis acknowledges the applause of his friends." (LJB.)

Bob Gainer is shown standing outside the Carter and Gainer Grocery, located at 3010 East Third Street, in this 1947 photograph. (GFC.)

This photograph, taken on August 29, 1964, is of Sanders Market at 301 East Fourth Street. For many years, S. E. Harsey, who came here in 1908, operated a gasoline station on this site. Harsey was one of the original voters to incorporate Millville. In 1912, Harsey operated the launch *Stanley* and other boats on St. Andrews Bay. (BCPL.)

This was the Millville Service Station it was located at 320 Parker Road, next to the Millville Advent Christian Church. The street was sometimes called the Millville-Parker Road, running east from Watsaw Bayou, two blocks south of the coastal highway (now U.S. Barreau 98). The Andersons lived in the back of the building. (JW.)

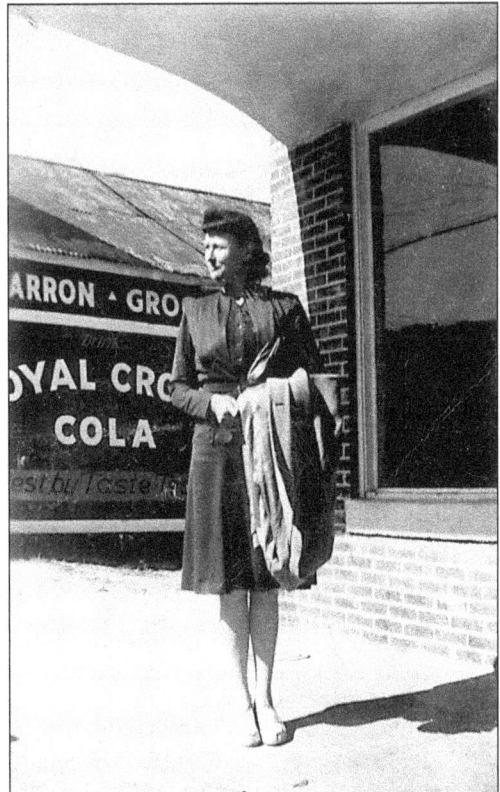

Postmistress Myrthel Gunther is standing in front of the Millville Post Office in 1941. The post office was located on Third Street next door to what is now Sweet Magnolias. She was the mother of Roberta (Billie) Blackwell of Millville. (KH.)

Boyette and Casey Hardware has served the public at the center of Millville since 1943. In this photograph, Hiram Porter is standing in the middle aisle. (FLC.)

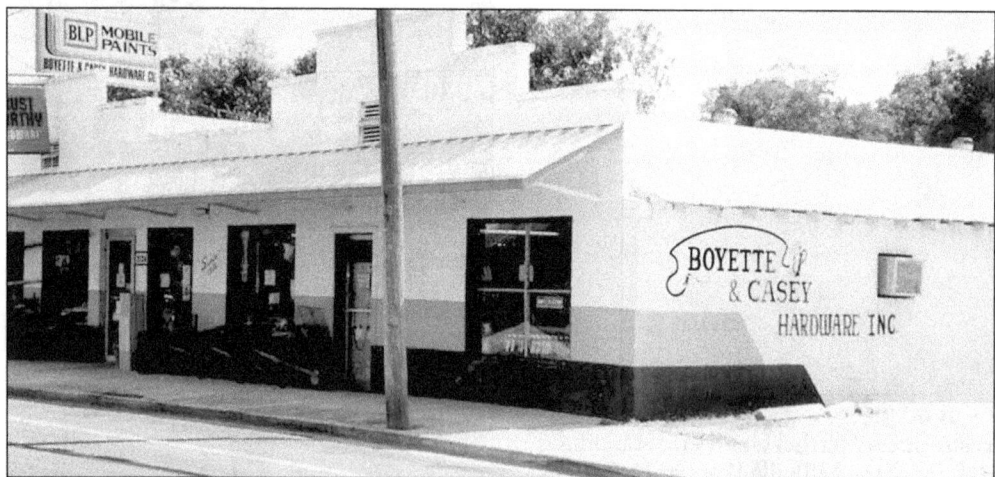

The hardware store has most anything needed for jobs around the home, and it is right there in the neighborhood. The building used to house a candy store owned by Sam Sawyer. There was a hardware store across the street. Sawyer bought it and established it in the candy store building. Boyette acquired the hardware business in 1943. (FLC.)

Shown here are Frederick Casey, who became a partner of Boyette and, in 1958, bought the store from him, and Casey's son, Fred L., who worked in the store, became a partner with his father, and now runs the business. (FLC.)

This article in the *Panama City News Herald* on September 27, 1968, was laminated and framed by the Caseys. It describes the friendly helpful service of the partners and points out all the items available, such as "gloves—for oystering, gardening, cement work and any other jobs— there are gloves to fit your need." Boyette and Casey has everything from little nails to a wood stove, including the rolls of cable the Caseys are standing in front of in the top picture. (AC.)

Gene's Oyster Bar on the corner of Sherman Avenue and Third Street in Millville may be the oldest oyster bar in Bay County. It is still a favorite today. (AC.)

This Hiram's Oyster Bar as it appeared when it belonged to Hiram Conrad, who opened the business in September 1935 on the corner of Sherman Avenue and Third Street. Hiram married Mamie Ruth Fleming on May 16, 1936. They had three children, Roy, Rita Ann, and Roderick Hiram. Hiram's oyster bar was one of 15 in the area and was the only one to survive. Eating oysters was a tradition at Conrad's, especially on opening day. He operated the oyster bar for 31 years until his death on November 23, 1966. Gene Bruner, who worked with Hiram, bought the oyster bar, and it is still open today. (RC.)

Rebecca Saunders, president of the Bay County Historical Society, presents a plaque to retired judge Fred Turner at the dedication of a marker at the Bay County Courthouse on August 5, 2003. The marker is in memory of the Gideon landmark case that established the public defender system across the United States. (BCPL.)

Clarence Earl Gideon's sons, David (left) and Ronald (right), meet retired-judge Fred Turner before the dedication of the marker at the Bay County Courthouse on August 5, 2003. Judge Turner was defense counsel for Gideon, who was appealing his conviction because he had not had a defense attorney. (BCPL.)

Bobbie Cotton Kochevar and her friend Diane Hall chat as they help with research for *Millville* on January 16, 2005. (AC.)

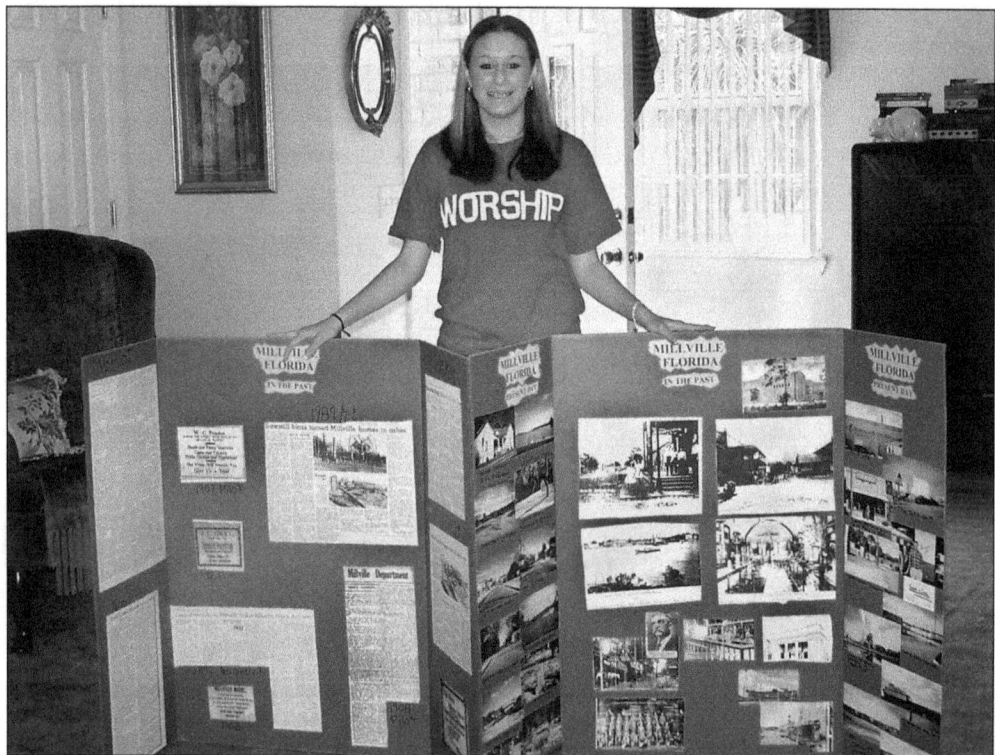

Diane Hall's granddaughter, Michelle, shows the backboards for her history project, which was on Millville. (AC.)

Six

COMMUNITY
REDEVELOPMENT

Motorists approaching the Glen Bridge when driving from Panama City into Millville can see more pleasure craft and sailboats anchored in Watson Bayou, as marina space around the waterfront dwindles. (AC.)

This is the former home of the late judge Fred Turner in Millville. It was built in 1914 at the corner of Center Avenue and Second Plaza. Mr. and Mrs. W. F. Turner acquired it in 1917 and owned it until 1950. Their children were James Henry, Verlie, Connie, Howard S., Lucille, Alma, Wallace N., and W. Fred. (BCPL.)

Sweet Magnolia's is a very popular lunch spot for the area located in the historic center of Millville, on Third Street near Sherman Avenue, along with Gene's Oyster Bar and Boyette and Casey Hardware. Sweet Magnolia's was open six years in downtown Panama City before moving to Millville in 1995. The building originally housed a drugstore—Troy Gilbert's Patents, Cigars and Sundries—and later Jake and Ivey Sims' Sundries. Today the restaurant is owned by Kathy Hanline and Sherry K. Groom. (AC.)

This is the Cotton home (seen on page 30) as it looks today with different owners. (CFC.)

This is Third Street in Millville today looking west toward Sherman Avenue. People are moving into Millville and restoring the old homes in many cases. Many Millville residents remain in their family "home place" hoping that when progress comes, it won't change the old community too much. Note the brick sidewalk, which is part of redevelopment. (AC.)

This house on Maine Street is the same one that was occupied by Ed and Wilhelmina Pratt in the early 1900s (page 28). Millville today is a progressive attractive community. (AC.)

This meeting of the Millville Community Alliance, presided over by James O'Shields, is an indication of community support and interest in revitalization of Millville. These residents want to make sure that they have input into the way progress will affect their lives. The *Panama City Pilot* article in 1908 spoke of a bright future for Millville. The members of the MCA want to ensure it in the 21st century. Also present at the meeting were Kathy Hanline, a Panama City commissioner and owner of Sweet Magnolia's, and Nancy Wengle, redevelopment director, along with other citizens. (AC.)

www.ingramcontent.com/pod-product-compliance
Lightning Source LLC
Chambersburg PA
CBHW050657110426
42813CB00007B/2038